destiny--so much so that we won't live our lives casually but with an understanding of You

we pray. God, help us discern Your divine purpose for our lives and to live in such a way that

thing on our lives as husband and wife than we could if we had not become one flesh in Your eye

of Your ways, governed by a wisdom that is from above rather than the wisdom that is of me

a way that we bring You pleasure. May we realize that You brought us together because we

h in Your eyes. Give us a sense of destiny--so much so that we won't live our lives casually

at is of men. In Your holy name, we pray. God, help us discern Your divine purpose for our li

ause we can better achieve Your calling on our lives as husband and wife than we could if we h

sually but with an understanding of Your ways, governed by a wisdom that is from above rat

e for our lives and to live in such a way that we bring You pleasure. May we realize that

ould if we had not become one flesh in Your eyes. Give us a sense of destiny--so much so tha

m above rather than the wisdom that is of men. In Your holy name, we pray. God, help us disc

at You brought us together because we can better achieve Your calling on our lives as husband a

that we won't live our lives casually but with an understanding of Your ways, governed b

us discern Your divine purpose for our lives and to live in such a way that we bring You pleasur

husband and wife than we could if we had not become one flesh in Your eyes. Give us a sense

rned by a wisdom that is from above rather than the wisdom that is of men. In Your holy na

g You pleasure. May we realize that You brought us together because we can better achieve Y

s a sense of destiny--so much so that we won't live our lives casually but with an understand

holy name, we pray. God, help us discern Your divine purpose for our lives and to live in su

eve Your calling on our lives as husband and wife than we could if we had not become one flesh

rstanding of Your ways, governed by a wisdom that is from above rather than the wisdom that

such a way that we bring You pleasure. May we realize that You brought us together because

flesh in Your eyes. Give us a sense of destiny--so much so that we won't live our lives casua

om that is of men. In Your holy name, we pray. God, hel purpose for

es because we can better achieve Your calling on our lives a we could if

ives casually but with an understanding of Your ways, go is from ab

rpose for our lives and to live in such a way that we bring easure. May we realize that help us discern in Your divine purpose for our lives and to live in such a way that we live... May we realize that You brought us together because we can better achieve Your call... lives as husband and wife than we could if we had not become one flesh in Your eyes. Give us a... sense of destiny... so that we won't live our lives casually but with an understanding of Your... and the wisdom that is from above rather than the wisdom that is of men. In Your holy... pray, God, help us discern Your divine purpose for our lives and to live in such a way that we... May we realize that You brought us together because we can better achieve Your... our lives as husband and wife than we could if we had not become one flesh in Your eyes. Give... of destiny, so much so that we won't live our lives casually but with an understanding... powered by a wisdom that is from above rather than the wisdom that is of men. In Your... we pray, God, help us discern Your divine purpose for our lives and to live in such a way... bring You glory... May we realize that You brought us together because we can better achieve... our lives as husband and wife than we could if we had not become one flesh in Y... a sense of destiny, so much so that we won't live our lives casually but with an unde... Your... ...led by a wisdom that is from above rather than the wisdom that is of men... ...God, help us discern Your divine purpose for our lives and to live in such... ...we bring You glory... May we realize that You brought us together because we can better... ...our lives as husband and wife than we could if we had not become one flesh... ...sense of destiny, so much so that we won't live our lives casually but...

KAY ARTHUR

PRAYERS TO BLESS YOUR *Marriage*

HARVEST HOUSE™ PUBLISHERS

EUGENE, OREGON

PRAYERS TO BLESS YOUR MARRIAGE

Copyright © 2003 by Kay Arthur
Published by Harvest House Publishers
Eugene, Oregon 97402
www.harvesthousepublishers.com

Library of Congress Cataloging-in-Publication Data

Arthur, Kay, 1933-
   Prayers to bless your marriage / Kay Arthur.
      p. cm.
   ISBN 0-7369-0700-9
   1.Marriage—Religious aspects—Christianity. 2. Spouses—Religious
life. I. Title.
   BV4596.M3 A79 2001
   248.4—dc21   2001024266

Design and Production by Koechel Peterson & Associates, Inc., Minneapolis, Minnesota

Verses are taken from the New American Standard Bible ®, © 1960, 1962, 1963, 1968,
1971, 1972, 1973, 1975, 1977, 1995 by The Lockman Foundation. Used by permission.

Printed in China.

03 04 05 06 07 08 09 10 11 / LP / 10 9 8 7 6 5 4 3 2 1

CONTENTS

INTRODUCTION

It's a moment in time.
A promise made.
A vow taken.

Then the words you've longed to hear—"I now pronounce you husband and wife."

The place where it happened is not as important as what happened. What happened is that you have said to whoever was present that you have made a choice. This is the man, the woman, with whom you have chosen to become one flesh, to live with in a way that you will not live with any other— as husband and wife.

This is the beginning of becoming a family...maybe just two, maybe more, but family. You belong to one another...

Sometimes we find ourselves feeling a little pensive; we catch ourselves musing about our life, wondering,

WHY WERE WE BORN?
WHAT IS OUR PURPOSE?
WHAT DOES OUR FUTURE HOLD?

We look at each other and wonder, "Why us?" Why out of all the people on the earth did we find one another, choose one another?

We cannot help wondering what it will be like for us not simply today but tomorrow and in the days that follow our tomorrows. How long will they be? What are the days that God has granted us as husband and wife? And how can we be sure that they are lived to the fullest? How can we discover all that He has designed for a marriage to be, His reason for bringing us together?

O God, HOW WE THANK YOU that Your book, the Bible, never leaves us in the dark—wondering, questioning—as to why we were born, why we are living, what the future holds, and why You ordained that a man and woman should become one flesh. You tell us in Your Word that You are the Creator of all things and that it is because of Your pleasure that we exist.

That is so hard to comprehend, that each of us would be brought into existence simply because it pleased You. Sometimes it is hard to fathom that You would even know about us individually, that the Creator of the universe has a purpose for us.

God, we come to You as Elohim—our Creator. Help us discern Your divine purpose for our lives and to live in such a way that we bring You pleasure. May we realize that You brought us together because we can better achieve Your calling on our lives as husband and wife than we could if we had not become one flesh in Your eyes.

Give us a sense of destiny—so much so that we won't live our lives casually but with an understanding of Your ways, governed by a wisdom that is from above rather than the wisdom that is of men.

Our world is so confused; relationships are fragile, fragmented, and fraught with pain.

We see and hear of so many marriages in turmoil. Protect us, Almighty God, from self-destructing. Help us to build such a strong marriage that we leave a legacy of righteousness, and that all will know our marriage was truly ordained by You. And when we come to the end of our days, may we look back and see that truly Your goodness and Your mercy have been with us all the days of our lives. May we, Father, have a marriage without regrets.

We ask all this, Father, in the light of Your promise that if we ask anything in Your name, You will do it.

The Mystery of MALE & FEMALE

We're different; we're not as alike as we thought we were.

Sometimes we find ourselves surprised by one another, the differences delightful and refreshing. "I never knew that about you!" The discovery is a treasure uncovered. But then there are other times, times, well, when we must admit our differences can be very frustrating—sometimes even disillusioning.

We wonder why—when it is so obvious that there is only one way to handle the situation properly, to respond to a person appropriately, to make a right decision—both of us don't see it, don't agree.

Situations like this can bring panic to our hearts, making us wonder secretly (even if we don't verbalize it) if we made a mistake, if we married the wrong person.

Thank God He has not left us in the dark as to these differences! They are explained in Genesis, the book of beginnings—

THE BEGINNING OF CREATION,
THE BEGINNING OF MAN,
THE BEGINNING OF MARRIAGE.

Then God said, "Let Us make man in Our image, according to Our likeness; and let them rule over the fish of the sea and over the birds of the sky and over the cattle and over all the earth, and over every creeping thing that creeps on the earth."

*God created man in His own image, in the image
of God He created him; male and female He created them.*

Genesis 1:26-27

Male and female. . . O FATHER, God our Creator,

the physical differences in us are so evident. So delightfully evident. It's obviously one of the reasons we were attracted to one another. And yet, at times, even that physical difference, that physical attraction, doesn't seem enough to override the differences that oftentimes become so frustratingly obvious.

It is hard at times to understand why we respond to one another as we do—with amazement, frustration, exasperation, and at times even, unfortunately, in anger, in disgust, and with harsh words…words sometimes so harsh that they are difficult to forget.

O God, we know You tell us that marriage is a permanent relationship, a covenant relationship. Help us to understand that although we are equal in Your eyes, there are differences between us.

Lord, teach us to understand and appreciate one another's differences and to delight in them, knowing that together we are more complete than we are apart. Help us to understand that woman was made to complete man, not to compete with him. Let us see our differences as assets rather than hindrances so that we move together in our strengths, valuing one another rather than being jealous or feeling inadequate in each other's shadow.

Help us, Father, define our roles as husband and wife according to Your Word rather than the world's ideas. Show us how we are to

RELATE TO ONE ANOTHER,
GIVE EACH OTHER SPACE,
HELP ONE ANOTHER,

and cherish and appreciate one another so that we can walk in the quiet confidence that comes from knowing we are honoring one another and our differences as You would have us do.

Thank You, our blessed Creator, for forming us in our mothers' wombs, designing us as man and woman so we might complete each other.

In Your holy name, we pray.

GOD BLESSED THEM; AND GOD SAID TO THEM,
"BE FRUITFUL AND MULTIPLY, AND FILL THE EARTH, AND SUBDUE IT;
AND RULE OVER THE FISH OF THE SEA AND OVER THE BIRDS OF THE
SKY AND OVER EVERY LIVING THING THAT MOVES ON THE EARTH."

Genesis 1:28

Then THE LORD GOD *formed man of dust from the ground, and breathed into his nostrils the breath of life; and man became a living being. The LORD God planted a garden toward the east, in Eden; and there He placed the man whom He had formed . . . Then the LORD God said, "It is not good for the man to be alone; I will make him a helper suitable for him." Out of the ground the LORD God formed every beast of the field and every bird of the sky, and brought them to the man to see what he would call them; and whatever the man called a living creature, that was its name. The man gave names to all the cattle, and to the birds of the sky, and to every beast of the field, but for Adam there was not found a helper suitable for him. So the LORD God caused a deep sleep to fall upon the man, and he slept; then He took one of his ribs and closed up the flesh at that place. The LORD God fashioned into a woman the rib which He had taken from the man, and brought her to the man.*

GENESIS 2:7-8, 18-22

❖

Sometimes our emotions overrule our minds.

We know what is right—the path we are to take, the response we should give—but we're so disappointed, angry, frustrated, or just downright mad that we simply don't want to do what is right.

Or we are tempted, so lured by the desire of our flesh that we want what we want when we want it even though it is forbidden, wrong, and destructive.

Can anything keep us from self-destructing? Rein in our passion? Restrain us from taking a path that violates God's precepts, His standards of morality, and the sanctity of marriage—and thus arouse the just judgment of God because we aren't honoring our marriage covenant?

The answer is yes if we will but desire and determine to honor God as God no matter the cost to our own personal desires. The secret to a strong marriage is our relationship to God. Marriage is often pictured in the form of a triangle. God is at the apex of the triangle, with man at one side of its base and woman on the other side. The closer each draws near to God, the closer each draws near to the other.

God, WE ARE ASKING YOU today to keep us ever mindful of how crucial it is that we give You preeminence in our lives. We know that only as You have first place in our lives will we be what we ought to be to one another and thus honor the covenant we made when we became man and wife. Help us to see that it is love of You and of Your Son that draws us to one purpose—to glorify You, to treat You as we should because of who You really are…El Shaddai, the Almighty God.

Father, help us to encourage one another to set aside time each day to be in Your Word, to be still and remember that You are God and that we don't live by bread alone but by every word that comes from Your mouth, every word in Your holy book, the Bible.

Show us how to order our days so that we discipline ourselves, giving adequate time for sleep and adequate time to begin our day with You by reading Your Word. We need Your Word for, as Jesus said, Your words are spirit and life.

> THOSE WHO HONOR ME I WILL HONOR, AND THOSE WHO DESPISE ME WILL BE LIGHTLY ESTEEMED.
> *1 Samuel 2:30*

May we see that every minute of quiet before You in Your Word and in prayer will make all the difference in our day and the way we view things. It will remind us of who You are and of Your precepts of life. Spending time with You will bring a sense of confidence, knowing that You are with us and will bless us with the wisdom and direction we need because we have honored You as God.

And, Father, help us to see the importance of praying together. What confidence, what strength it imparts when we hear each other talk to You. May we remember You are not impressed with our eloquence but with our sincerity, even though our petitions and praise come forth in halting, stumbling words. Even as parents do not despise the words of their children as they learn to talk, so You do not despise or demean our stammering. You simply delight in the fact that we would take the time to come together to commit our ways to You, to trust in You, to tell You that we do not want to lean to our own understanding but in all of our ways to acknowledge You so that You, the Almighty God, might direct our paths.

Precious Father, may we see You as that—a father who is so precious to us that we want to give You the honor due You as our Father, listening to You and

SEEKING YOUR HELP,
YOUR PROVISION, YOUR WISDOM,
AND YOUR COUNSEL,

and then living accordingly. May we understand that to ignore You, to try to make it on our own, is not only foolish but also debilitating to ourselves and to our marriage. May we strengthen our marriage and ourselves as individuals by honoring You as God day by day, listening to Your Word and communicating with You in prayer.

We ask this all in the name that is above every name, the name of Your only begotten Son, the Son of man, the Lord Jesus Christ.

Leaving the Past
BEHIND

Sometimes our relationship with our parents, if not viewed correctly, can greatly hamper our relationship with each other.

Because we live in a society that has forgotten God and that has lost its fear of God—a respect and trust of Him for who He really is—we often come from fractured families. Consequently, not only is our understanding of marriage often distorted, but our souls are scarred by the trauma of living in unwholesome situations.

Because of this distortion, each of us may bring a lot of baggage into our marriage. We can have a tendency to misread the actions, the words, and even the body language of one another. An abused puppy can shy away from a hand that means only to caress it!

When one of us acts a certain way, speaks a certain way, responds in a certain way, or even looks a certain way, the other often connects it to something someone else did in the past. Without thinking, we assume the other person is acting just like the parent who disappointed us, misused us, demeaned us, wounded us. We attribute to our mate what we suppose was meant rather than what was really meant.

How destructive this can be to our relationship when we don't give one another the benefit of the doubt, but rather accuse each other of emotions, attitudes, or feelings that we really don't have.

How crucial it is, therefore, that we always ask rather than assume what each other's attitude or intentions are, and how vital it is that when we ask for clarification of one another's words or actions, we accept what our loved one says unless he or she demonstrates otherwise. What grace and wisdom this requires from above.

O Lord God, WHEN YOU FASHIONED the

woman from the rib You had taken from the man and brought her to the man, You said, "For this reason a man shall leave his father and his mother and shall be joined to his wife." Help us to see and understand the priority of our relationship as husband and wife over our relationship to our parents—to understand that to cleave is to join together in a permanent way, even as two things are superglued together so they are no longer two, but one. Glue us together, God, as one. Show us how to honor our parents and yet give priority to one another as we build our home and our family.

> HEAL ME, O LORD, AND I WILL BE HEALED. SAVE ME AND I WILL BE SAVED, FOR YOU ARE MY PRAISE.
> *Jeremiah 17:14*

And, Father, in the leaving and cleaving, if our relationship with our parents has not been a healthy one, one in which our parents honored You by loving us and raising us in accordance with Your Word, may we leave that behind. May we learn how to let it go and be healed. Keep us from misunderstanding each other, challenging or withdrawing from one another, because we are projecting on our loved one what was done to us by another.

Teach us to honestly and gently communicate with one another, to trust each other so that we can unravel our bandages and share our wounds. Then together may we seek Your healing as our Jehovah Rapha, the Lord God who heals.

<h2 style="text-align:center">WE CAN NEVER CHANGE THE PAST.
IT'S OVER, DONE, GONE.</h2>

Therefore to focus on what is past will bring us nothing but grief. It will keep us from pressing on to all that You want us to be as individuals and in the oneness of our marriage. You promise us, Father, that You will use the past for our good, that You will use it to make us more like Christ. May we believe You and move forward in our relationship as husband and wife, developing a oneness that nothing and no one can divide.

Thank You for being our God, our Jehovah Rapha.

Creating a Little Bit of
HEAVEN ON EARTH

Home—

whether a trailer

> *or one-room apartment,*

a small two-bedroom house in a common neighborhood where all the houses are the same, lined neatly in a row, street after street,

> *or the house of your dreams in the upscale subdivision you've always wanted to live in—*

HOME IS TO BE YOUR SANCTUARY.

We all long for a sanctuary, a place of security, of safety, of refuge from the world with all its pressures and its stress. A place where we feel secure—where we know we are loved and appreciated by at least one other person.

Home is to be a place where heaven meets earth…

O Father, WHEN WE THINK OF HEAVEN,

we think of a place of peace. A place of joy. A place of acceptance.

You tell us in Ephesians 3 that You are the source, the pattern from which every family in heaven and earth derives its name. You are the eternal Father. It is obvious in Jesus' prayer that there is such a oneness in Your family, that there is no discord between You, Your Son, and the Spirit. We know from reading the Gospels that You appreciate one another and respect one another's roles, and that Your mission is to make Your family complete by drawing us to Yourself—and promising us that one day we'll all live together in heaven, our Father's home.

O Father of fathers, show us how to build a home within our house that will give our children, our family, and our friends a small taste of heaven. We know that heaven is a prepared place—it didn't happen just by chance. Rather there is a design, a purpose to all that takes place there. It's a place of peace and righteousness—"nothing unclean, and no one who practices abomination and lying, shall ever come into it, but only those whose names are written in the Lamb's book of life" (Revelation 21:27).

Father, help us to strive by Your Spirit to make our home a place of peace, a place of serenity rather than confusion, disharmony, and discord. Show us how, in the busyness of life, to order our days and labor together so that our home is a place of quiet order. Let us be content with less when it comes to material things so that we can enjoy more of each other.

May our homes be places of righteousness. You command us to be holy even as You are holy. Therefore, may we determine that we will not permit or even watch things that would be displeasing to You. May the language spoken in our home, the stories told, the books on our shelves, and the magazines on our tables be edifying rather than destructive. May nothing that would pollute our minds or destroy us morally be permitted within our home.

And, O Father, may we determine that we will treat each other and talk to each other with respect and kindness, knowing that each of us was created by You and for You and that when we don't honor one another we are dishonoring You.

May love reign in our home as it does in Yours. Help us to realize the importance of relationships. Of valuing one another. Of listening. Of communicating. When our loved one comes home, may we make it "an abundant entrance" as your Word tells us we will receive when someday we enter into heaven itself. Remind us to greet one another with pleasure rather than criticism, complaints, or commands. Make us sensitive to one another's needs. May our home be a place where tears are wiped away,

WHERE SORROW AND PAIN ARE ASSUAGED, WHERE COMFORT ABOUNDS.

Father, in the rush and stress of life, may we seek out ways to make our home a place of restoration. May we demonstrate to others what You meant a home to be. May we give them a taste of paradise, a foretaste of what heaven is like so that all long to know the Savior whom we love and serve.

I am my beloved's and my beloved is mine . . .

To know and experience unconditional love is the longing of every person's heart, and it is the desire of our hearts to know and experience this love as husband and wife. Oh, the security, the wholeness, the confidence, the liberty it brings to our being to know that we are the most important person on earth to our mate. This is a divine love—an overriding love that seeks the other's very highest good. This is the love we want to give to one another...love drawn from the heart of God...

Father, YOU ARE SUCH AN ENCOURAGER, the God of all hope, One who loves us and delights in us. As we read Your Word, it becomes obvious that we are very precious in Your sight—

LOVED WITH AN EVERLASTING LOVE,
DRAWN TO YOU IN LOVING-KINDNESS,
ACCEPTED IN THE BELOVED, CHOSEN BY YOU.

You lavish Your extravagant grace—unearned, unmerited—upon us out of the goodness of Your heart, out of the selfless desire for us to reach our full potential in You. Your intentions toward us, even when we falter and fail, are always kind. You always desire our highest good. How we thank You! What manner of love You have bestowed upon us that we should be Your children! That we should be the bride of Your Son, the Lord Jesus Christ!

Truly, as Your Word says, "in Your presence is fullness of joy; in Your right hand there are pleasures forevermore" (Psalm 16:11).

Such love, such delight, attracts us to You as a moth to the light.

O Father, may we in turn follow Your example. We know that what makes us winsome and attractive to others is the way they feel about themselves when they are with us.

Show us how to make others feel good about who they are. Show us ways to bring our loved one joy. Let us learn to be fun.

ENTHUSIASTIC. ENCOURAGERS.
OPTIMISTIC RATHER THAN PESSIMISTIC.

After all, You are the God of all hope! In one of her darkest hours, You told your wife Israel in the book of Jeremiah that the plans You had for her were plans for welfare and not for calamity to give her a future and a hope. Teach us to convey that same hope, that same sense of a good and secure future to one another.

Help us learn to emulate You in our relationship. Teach us ways to make our marriage a delight. Show us how to bring joy to one another. To build each other up rather than tear down and destroy. To increase one another's confidence. Even as You first loved us, may we race to "first love" one another, knowing that we are never more like You, Father, than when we take love's initiative—even when one of us is in a foul mood or a defeated state. Help us to think, Lord, of how Your Son responds to His bride, the church, when she is not all that she ought to be and do the same.

O Father, mentor us in the art of selfless love…

Building a Strong,
UNBREAKABLE RELATIONSHIP

There are so many voices, so many opinions on our roles as husbands and wives.

How we need to be assured that the road we take is the one that ends in life rather than death. We know the world doesn't have the answers. It's blatantly obvious as we hear the statistics with respect to divorce. So many of our business associates, fellow workers, friends, and acquaintances are confused, pulled in every direction—and some have been emotionally drawn and quartered. Their relationships are fractured. Their lives and homes have disintegrated. They permitted the world to squeeze them into its mold, and the pressure became so great they shattered into a thousand pieces. It's scary. We don't want that to happen to us. We don't want to ignore the precepts, the standards, God set for us to live by.

Almighty God, ELOHIM, You are the One who began the institution of marriage. You are the One who created us male and female. The One who wrote the script for our roles as husband and wife. If in any way we have been blindsided by the world and have embraced its philosophies and morals, forgive us and help us. We believed a lie, we missed truths. O Father, teach us Your precepts; give us understanding that we might restrain our feet from every evil way. Through Your Word help us to understand what is right in Your eyes and then lead us in paths of righteousness for Your name's sake.

HUSBANDS, LOVE YOUR WIVES, *just as Christ also loved the church and gave Himself up for her, so that He might sanctify her, having cleansed her by the washing of water with the Word, that He might present to Himself the church in all her glory, having no spot or wrinkle or any such thing; but that she would be holy and blameless.*

So husbands ought also to love their own wives as their own bodies. He who loves his own wife loves himself; for no one ever hated his own flesh, but nourishes and cherishes it, just as Christ also does the church, because we are members of His body.

For this reason a man shall leave his father and mother and shall be joined to his wife; and the two shall become one flesh. This mystery is great; but I am speaking with reference to Christ and the church. Nevertheless, each individual among you also is to love his own wife even as himself; and the wife must see to it that she respects her husband.

EPHESIANS 5:25-33

When we read that classic passage in the New Testament from the fifth chapter of Ephesians, it is so clear that the greater responsibility falls upon the broad shoulders of the husband, for God commands the husband to love his wife in the same way Jesus loves the church. The word for love, agape, *is that which is unconditional, desiring the other's highest good. This is not reciprocal love, nor is it one of friendship born of admiration and delight—rather it is a sacrificial love. It is the love bestowed on mankind when we were God's enemies—helpless, hopeless—sinners. It's the love that designed Calvary. It's the love of sacrifice demonstrated on a cross.*

A *Husband's* PRAYER

O God, You make it so clear how unconditionally I am to love my wife. Her needs come before mine. Her welfare before mine. I am to lay down my life for her even as Jesus laid down His life for me.

You tell me that I'm to love my wife as I would myself, as I would my very own body. That which is not perfect in her—the spots and blemishes as You call them—are not to deter love. Rather I am to nourish her—to do all I can to bring her to the full potential as a mature women of God. Such love compels me to protect her…to cherish her.

Keep me from devaluing her through criticism or scorn. As a man, a husband, You have asked me to make her feel so cherished, so needed, so valued that she will walk in the confidence and security of my love. May I so tenderly care for my wife that she blossoms into all that a woman can be when she's secure in the love of her husband.

O God, I know what I am—and I know that my focus quickly leans toward myself. You ask much from us as husbands—and it is so contrary to the way many of the men around me live. Help me keep the example of Your Son before me. Help me remember the way I want to be loved and treated. Help me—when I think of myself, what I want, what will nourish me, what will benefit me—to remember that the bottom line of my relationship with my wife is love. Loving her sacrificially and loving her as I love myself.

Father, help my wife to be patient with me…to encourage me…for I do want to fulfill the role You have for me as a husband to my wife.

I ask all this in the name of Your Son, who lived and died for me…and gave me His example to follow and the power to do it through the indwelling Holy Spirit.

WIVES, BE SUBJECT TO YOUR OWN HUSBANDS, *as to the Lord. For the husband is the head of the wife, as Christ also is the head of the church, He himself being the Savior of the body. But as the church is subject to Christ, so also the wives ought to be to their husbands in everything. . .Nevertheless, each individual among you also is to love his own wife even as himself; and the wife must see to it that she respects her husband.*

EPHESIANS 5:22-24, 33

So often as women we hear that we are to submit to our husbands apart from the context of the verses in Ephesians 5 which address the husband. "Submit" would be a word that would cause any woman to shudder, to want to run away. To unequivocally submit to one's husband can strike fear in a wife's heart, for all the "what ifs" come immediately to mind.

Our primary need as women is to know that we are loved unconditionally. We were made for love, not just for sex, and sometimes it is so hard for men to understand the difference, especially when we live in a society that is so focused on the bedroom.

Yet when we read God's Word together, when we both stop to observe exactly what God is saying and think through the ramifications of such behavior, we see His commandments are so reasonable, so perfect in creating the harmony and oneness we desire as husband and wife.

A *Wife's* PRAYER

O God, You have placed such great responsibility on my husband's shoulders. It's obvious that You value me as a woman. Now, Father, I want to do my part—to fulfill my role as a wife.

I know that the command to submit is given to me. It is not my husband's responsibility to make me submit; rather I am to submit as unto You. To not do so would be disobedience. How I thank You that when I heed Your voice to be filled with the Holy Spirit submission will be the outcome of that filling—submitting to one another in love.

Lord, I don't always understand my husband, but it is apparent because You have made him my head that to refuse to submit would only challenge the role You ordained for him. May he never fear that he is being ruled over by his wife.

You have made me a helper, a partner to my husband. I know that my opinion, my insights, my intuition as a woman, and my discernment are valuable to him—and that being submissive does not mean I cannot share these things.

I understand that I am of value and play a significant role in our marriage. Therefore it is my joy, Almighty God, to obey You and arrange myself under my husband and to give him the respect he needs.

Father, I would never want to risk damaging my husband's self-esteem. Like all men, his ego can be very tender at times. So show me ways to build him up and let him know how very special he is in my eyes as well as Yours.

Help me now to be everything You intend for me to be. I love You, Father, and I want to demonstrate that by the way I treat my husband. Thank You for the gift of the Holy Spirit. Fill me now…

Overcoming the
WORRY OF FINANCES

The end of the month is never fun.

Finances are one of the hardest things we have to deal with as a couple. We came into our marriage with different attitudes about money. One of us wants to spend freely, to buy what we want and then figure out how we're going to pay for it later. The other one is so cautious, so careful, so frugal with money that we find it one of the major areas of contention. We were just raised differently.

On top of all this, there is always the issue of the economy. Sometimes the future can be scary. We wonder if we are going to make it financially—if the job will be there, if there will be layoffs, if there is enough money in the bank to survive even a month, if we'll be able to pay our debts, if we should go into debt, if we're going to save enough to meet future expenses. What if we got sick…what if…

On and on it goes. We worry about tomorrow and on top of all that we have to deal with today. And with it all comes incredible tension, stress. Sometimes even accusations about wanting too much,

SPENDING TOO MUCH,
UNWISE PURCHASES,
INVESTMENTS—DO WE, DON'T WE, WHY DID YOU?
CREDIT CARDS.

Disagreements over what is important—where the money ought to go, how it ought to be spent. God help us. It's hard on our relationship.

O God, OUR JEHOVAH JIREH, the One who supplies all our needs, we come to You because we need Your help. We need Your words, Your wisdom, Your direction. You know the tension finances can bring to our marriage—You know the things we say to each other out of fear, anger, or pressure, or because of mistakes we've made with our money.

Help us, Father. We know conflict over finances shipwrecks many marriages. Obviously You know this and You have the answers we need, so quiet our hearts as we seek You in this aspect of our marriage.

Your Word makes it clear that not only are You the source, but You are also the provider of everything we need. If anything ought to give us confidence in uncertain times, in times of distress, it ought to be this. According to Your Word, You are the One who makes rich and who makes poor, who humbles and lifts up. Every good and perfect gift comes down from You—the earth is Yours and the fullness thereof, and we believe that. And You are the One who promises to supply *all* our needs according to Your riches in glory in Your Son, Jesus Christ. In the light of that, Father, if we are Yours, then fear of the future, fear of what we shall eat, drink, or put on, should not be part of our lives. You tell us that You know we have need of these things.

You also tell us, Father, that we are not to be preoccupied with wealth. Rather we are to seek first Your kingdom and Your righteousness and, as You say in Matthew 6, all these things will be added to us. Help us to remember this when we start to panic about the future. When we listen to financial predictions, help us to listen carefully and then bring what we hear to You in prayer. For it is You alone who knows what the future holds.

Father, take us to the book of Proverbs and give us Your wisdom on finances. Let us be of one mind in respect to the subject and determined that we will let You guide us in this fragile issue of money. Help us remember the importance of oneness in the area of finances and the need to discuss this openly and gently, to talk about these things, and to listen carefully so that we truly understand one another. And if either of us goes behind the other's back and deceptively spends money, may we realize that we are only hurting ourselves and our marriage—denying our oneness and possibly bringing us into a financial crisis we could have avoided.

Father, make clear to us whether it is important for us to work two jobs so we can live in a bigger home and give our children more material things or whether it is better to sacrifice, to live if necessary with a lot less, and give our children the undivided attention of a mother who devotes herself to the most important calling and career she could ever have—that of being a homemaker, wife, and mother without all the tension of holding down another job.

O God, in all of our concern about finances don't let us forget that You tell us we are to work in order to have money to help others to further the work of Your kingdom. You could pour money from heaven, but that is not the way You have chosen. You ordained to do it through the hands of Your children. May we pore over Your Word with wisdom, seeking until we understand the importance of giving. Then when we give, may we give with wisdom, seeking Your direction, fully aware that it is an honor and privilege to participate in the ministry of giving. May our motive never be to give in order to get, but to give out of obedience to You. You tell us we will have the poor with us always, so when we give may we make sure that we don't take care of a person's physical needs and leave them spiritually destitute.

In the light of all this, teach us how to discipline ourselves to live within our means. Help us to understand the destructiveness of purchasing things we cannot pay for and the utter wastefulness and folly of constantly paying interest on the debt we have incurred. Rather, teach us to plan, budget, and save so that we will be faithful stewards, as the Bible says, and not be a burden to others. Also help us to see the importance of wisely preparing for tomorrow.

Father, as we look at finances, may we look at them in the light of our priorities, our calling, and what is of real value. May we remember that marriages and families rarely suffer for the lack of material possessions; rather they suffer when their relationships are overstressed or torn in two by the quest for more—more of anything that keeps us from developing and strengthening our marriage and family. May we realize that to know true love and companionship in the midst of little is far better than suffering the abject poverty of experiencing prosperity and fame and finding ourselves alone and unloved.

O Father, all of this to simply say that we want to know how to handle our finances in a way that will please You and thus bring us the greatest peace and contentment we can know.

Discovering Sexual
SATISFACTION

To give yourself completely, totally, to each other—

to express love in a way that brings a physical oneness of the deepest kind—this is God's design…an act of beauty, of pleasure shared, an ecstacy beyond exquisite, a closeness beyond close. You have given, you have received—you have become one flesh with each other in every sense of the word. And it is as God intended.

What a treasure to guard. What a relationship to protect.

We are so bombarded by sex on every side that sometimes we feel terribly inadequate and frustrated. We find ourselves standing before the world's mirror and comparing our bodies, our physical relationship with all we see and hear. And we just want to turn out the lights, crawl into bed, say goodnight, and pull the covers over our heads.

All the infidelity of our friends, the terrible stories of addictions to pornography, sexual escapades on the Internet, and husbands and wives contracting sexually transmitted diseases can strike fear in our hearts. Will we remain faithful to one another?

And then come the issues of tiredness, lack of privacy, our crazy schedules. It seems that we are not really enjoying one another as we should when our sexual relationship, we are told, is so vital to a strong and healthy marriage.

O God, how we need Your help and protection.

Father, WE'VE COME TO TALK to You about our sexual relationship. All sorts of thoughts and feelings are running through our minds right now in respect to this subject. It is difficult to talk about it, to pray about it. For sex carries such an aura with it. It happens. It is seen as the magic of marriage that simply appears like a genie out of a bottle, satisfying all of our desires. But according to Your Word, this is not true. Sex is fragile, delicate—to be handled with care for there is so much involved in this physical union designed by You.

We realize that what we think about the subject, what we feel about it, and how we respond to one another has to do with our sexual history—before marriage and after marriage. What we know about sex has been communicated to us, sometimes pleasantly, sometimes unpleasantly, but rarely biblically. You know where we're at. You are God; nothing has ever been hidden from Your sight. Even the darkness is light to You. No one flees from Your presence.

God, thank You for being the great Redeemer. For being able to take our past, our sexual history, and redeem it for our good and for Your glory. Thank You for healing, for forgiving, and for cleansing and clearing our consciences if any of this is necessary. We come to You together, today, now, to tell You that we want to be whole and healthy in this vital aspect of our marriage.

First, we want to acknowledge that You are the One who designed us as sexual beings. "Male and female" is no accident; our sexuality was determined by you. Psalm 139 tells us that You formed us in our mothers' wombs. And we want to acknowledge that right now. We accept what You made us. We accept the way You made us. Therefore, while how we look and how sexually attractive we are is deemed so important in our society, we promise You that we will not compare our attractiveness, our prowess, our sexual attributes with anyone else.

Dear Lord, help us guard our sexual relationship as we would guard our own lives. This is the one unique gift we can give to each other, the unique experience we will share with no other. This is our vow as husband and wife. Yet, Father, it is more than that. This is an expression of our love that we will not neglect. Yet if it does not always bring us the pleasure, the ecstasy we desire, may we not withhold it from one another. May sexual oneness be our means of drawing close to each other, our way of showing our deepest commitment to our marriage.

Father, You tell us very clearly in 1 Corinthians 7 that we are to fulfill our sexual responsibility to one another: "The wife does not have authority over her own body…and likewise also the husband does not have authority over his own body, but the wife does." You make it clear we are not to deprive one another sexually unless it is to give ourselves to fasting and prayer…but then only for a limited time "so that Satan will not tempt us by our lack of self control." In other words, Lord, if we deny each other sexually, then we are putting one another in a vulnerable position and we will be held accountable because we are disobeying You. We don't want to do that, Lord.

Sex can be so satisfying to our own body that sometimes it is hard to consider the needs of the other person. We think that if we are satisfied our mate is satisfied, and that is not always the case. Or we think if we can do without it, then so can the other person. How wrong this is! Keep us sensitive to one another's needs.

Father, if we are not enjoying the sexual aspect of marriage or are not participating in it, help us to honestly look at our lifestyle and discover what is hindering us. If it's a lack of privacy, then may we make a concerted effort to change that. If it is a matter of busyness, then may we readjust our schedules, knowing that to neglect sex is to weaken our relationship and to put each other in a vulnerable situation.

If it is a lack of interest, then let us examine how much sleep we are getting, for tired people are usually too tired for sex. Help us to turn off the television, to let things wait until tomorrow if we are tired and it is late. May we remember that being in one another's arms revives us physically and emotionally, energizing our bodies and revitalizing our relationship.

Father, teach us to excel in the art of loving and appreciating one another. When we read the Song of Solomon, it is so evident that You designed us for this pleasure in the beauty of marriage. "I am my beloved's and his desire is for me." May our love for each other be as a seal over our hearts.

We ask this in the name of the One who calls us beloved.

We are so different sexually. We know God made us this way. Therefore, these are our prayers for each other.

A *Wife's* PRAYER

FATHER, I WANT TO PRAY FOR MY HUSBAND. *I know that when he is satisfied sexually, he is, as You say, like a bridegroom coming out of his chamber rejoicing as a strong man to run his course. It takes so much energy to have sex, but I know that in the expanding of his energies he is energized. Renewed. His manhood is confirmed. And it bonds us in such a precious and powerful way. Even when I lack the desire, may I meet his. May I do it as an offering to You out of obedience to You and out of dedication and understanding to him. Keep me from self-centeredness.*

Help me also remember that men are turned on by sight and therefore keep myself attractive in my husband's eyes according to what appeals to him. And also help me to remember that praising him rather than demeaning him not only strengthens him as a man but makes me far more desirable as a woman. Help me to give my husband the attention and companionship he needs.

May I remember You created me a woman because it is not good for man to be alone. So may I listen to him, sit with him, and affirm him not only in his role as my husband but also as my lover, for I know men respond to encouragement—they love to be someone's hero…may my husband know that he is mine.

A *Husband's* PRAYER

GOD, AS A HUSBAND, help me to understand this woman You have given me as my wife. Sometimes I am so eager to know the satisfaction of becoming one flesh I forget she is turned on by touch rather than by sight. Help me to consider her in my passion. I know that there is a stewardship connected with marriage. Therefore I need to be patient and understanding. Help me watch her carefully when we are in bed together, help me discern that which delights her and that which prepares her to enjoy our intimacy to the fullest.

Remind me that how I treat her during the day will determine how receptive she is to me when we go to bed. Help me learn to conduct myself in such a way that she won't think the only reason I want to hold her or kiss her is so I can have sex. Teach me to be tender and loving—to love her in ways *that appeal to her. I know that she would rather have me discover it for myself than have to tell me. Teach me my wife's love language, that which touches her heart. Is it flowers or a single rose?*

A BEAUTIFUL CARD,
A NOTE, A PHONE CALL?

An unexpected present that shows her I was thinking of her and made the effort? You know, God; I don't—but don't let me become weary before I discover what says "I love you" in a way that is special to her.

Help me remember how important words are to a woman. Words and courtesies like opening the door, getting out of my chair, putting down the newspaper. O Father, remind me of our differences so that she knows when I take her to our bed it's because she is the only one I want to be with. With her I am safe, accepted, satisfied. I don't need to perform, and neither does she. To be together, to be one flesh, is enough. Thank You, God, for the understanding You are going to give me.

I ask it all in the name of the One who understands me, Your Son, the Lord Jesus Christ.

Learning to Talk to ONE ANOTHER

We know that both of us, simply as human beings, have a need for a sense of security—

the guarantee of acceptance, of love…especially from one another. We need to know we have worth as individuals—and that our lives as a man and as a woman count for something; there is a purpose for our existence, for our marriage.

And how do we affirm this to one another? By talking. By listening. By caring enough to communicate. We communicate in so many different ways. Sometimes with a look and other times with a touch. Yet in our marriage, there needs to be words. We need to hear each other's voice, what the other is

THINKING, FEELING, DEALING WITH, DREAMING OF.

The way we communicate with one another can make a difference in whether our marriage is strong or weak, one of joy or of pain, one of health and wholeness or destruction. It is all in the art of communication, and it literally permeates every aspect of our marriage.

One of us loves to talk. The other is quieter. However, because healthy communication is critical to our relationship, we need to do whatever it takes to learn to communicate in an effective way. Nothing else shows more clearly that we truly care for and value our loved one above ourselves.

How we need to learn to listen to one another. To permit and encourage honesty, openness, vulnerability. To exchange thoughts, ideas, hopes, dreams, fears, and failures with one another in such a way that we free each other to share without fear, rejection, or judgment. When we talk in this way, it bonds us at a new and deeper level. And it gives us the courage to work out the issues we face as husband and wife in order to meet the future together with confidence. This is the life-support system of the strong and unshakable marriage we desire.

Father, WE KNOW THAT all creation came into existence because You spoke. Your book, the Bible, is Your Word. We exist because You communicated. We know what to believe and how to live because of Your words recorded and preserved in the Scriptures. We know that You spoke long ago "to the fathers in the prophets in many portions and in many ways" and that "in these last days" You have "spoken to us in Your Son."

You are the master communicator. Thus we come to You, to be instructed and taught by You, our Father God, in the art of communicating effectively with the one You have given us. You made us. You know our communication styles. You also know that when we speak to each other, what we say, what we hear, and how we respond are all filtered through our past experiences, our personalities, the background canvas of our lives. Therefore, we don't always hear correctly what is being said. In the light of this, help us to learn to talk, to question, to understand, and to believe what our loved one is saying to us rather than presuming things that are not true simply because we read our partner wrong or we project on them what is not reality.

Help us to be patient with one another, to talk things out rather than getting angry and stubbornly, defensively closing up. Let us see that understanding one another is vital to a marriage without regrets. Otherwise we can be deceived by a lie, misdirected by a perception, or disillusioned by a misconception. Soften our hearts, fill them with compassion, and cause us to be more concerned for our loved one than we are for ourselves. Let us understand we are in the process of building a relationship that will carry us safely through any storm or crisis of life, bringing us closer and closer to each other—

OF ONE MIND, ONE HEART, AND ONE SPIRIT.

Father, whenever we communicate, help us to uphold the priority of our marriage, permitting no other relationship to weaken ours. May the word "divorce" never be formed on our tongue, never pronounced with our lips. May it never be considered as a viable option—for it strikes terror in the heart, fear and anger in the mind, and anxiety to our souls. And it grieves Your holy heart.

May we always, in all our conversations, uphold the oneness of our marriage, understanding that what affects one always affects the other.

May we allow open and honest communication, encourage vulnerability and authenticity. May we never be guilty of breaking each other's spirit. Rather, may we affirm and strengthen one another so that together we can endure any weakness, any failure and not lose hope.

Father, help us to sharpen our communication skills. Teach us to communicate with our eyes—to convey our delight in the other's presence, to say "I love you," to let our loved one know even in a crowded room, "You're special to me." Remind us to give each other the gift of our full attention when we talk.

Teach us to respond to what is said so that our mate knows he or she is being heard. Help us to keep a confidence, to build a wall of trust so that we are free to share all that is in our hearts. And as we listen, Lord, help us to avoid giving quick or pat answers. Help us to listen patiently. Remind us that our loved one does not always want advice. Sometimes we just want to be heard, to say it, and to get it off our chest.

> OUR WORDS ARE OF SUCH SIGNIFICANCE, SUCH POWER THAT GOD TELLS US, DEATH AND LIFE ARE IN THE POWER OF THE TONGUE.
>
> *Proverbs 18:21*

Father, may we feel the freedom to open up and share our fears. Sometimes it is so difficult to admit weakness or fear, but we need to be able to talk to someone—and of all people, it should be our spouse. May we also know that we don't always have to dispel each other's fear—nor should we think we must have the cure. May we just learn to listen…listen and pray.

Father, we all need to have that sense of significance, of worth, of security, so teach us to continually look for ways, for words in private and in public, to build our loved one's self-esteem. When one of us shares with the other, may we learn not to attack each other verbally. May the goal of all our conversations be for the building up of one another, the healing of one another, and the encouragement of one another so our loved one will want to talk, to communicate. May our words never be demeaning or destructive.

And finally, Father, when our tempers flare, may we make it a practice not to lay our heads on our pillows and close our eyes until we have resolved our anger. You tell us very clearly, "Be angry, and yet do not sin; do not let the sun go down on your anger, and do not give the devil an opportunity."

As we look at the one lying on the pillow beside us, may we remember that this is the one to whom we made our vows to love in sickness and in health, for richer or poorer, for better or worse until death do us part.

Help us realize, Father, that a marriage like the one we prayed for is a marriage that speaks to all the world of the power and indestructible joy of living in obedience to the Word of God. A marriage demonstrates to the world that with You it is possible to have a marriage without regrets. A marriage that gives others a snapshot of the marriage of the Lamb and the heavenly home You have prepared for us.

The TONGUE REVEALS *what is in the wellspring of*

one's heart, whether the water is bitter or sweet. With our tongue…

We bless our Lord and Father, and with it we curse men,

who have been made in the likeness of God;

from the same mouth come both blessing and cursing.

My brethren, these things ought not to be this way.

Does a fountain send out from the same opening

both fresh and bitter water?

Can a fig tree, my brethren, produce olives, or a vine produce figs?

Nor can salt water produce fresh.

Who among you is wise and understanding?

Let him show by his good behavior his deeds

in the gentleness of wisdom.

JAMES 3:9–13

THE LORD BLESS YOU, AND KEEP YOU;

THE LORD MAKE HIS FACE SHINE ON YOU,

AND BE GRACIOUS TO YOU;

THE LORD LIFT UP HIS COUNTENANCE ON YOU,

AND GIVE YOU PEACE.

Numbers 6:24-26